THE RIGHTS OF CHILDREN.

THE

RIGHTS OF CHILDREN

IN

SPIRIT, MIND, AND BODY.

———

Thoughts for Parents.

———

BY

FRANCES S. HALLOWES.

———

London:

S. W. PARTRIDGE & CO.,

8 & 9, PATERNOSTER ROW.

—

1896.

PREFACE

——

THESE few thoughts upon the Rights of Children are addressed to parents; to *fathers* as well as to *mothers*. In these days there seems to be frequent abdication of their duties on the part of fathers; they persuade themselves that the right person to bear the burden of the spiritual, mental, and physical training of their children is the mother. To such may be pointed out the fact that the divine commands in God's Word are laid upon *fathers*, and it is they who are to be responsible for the nurture of their children.* This being the case, it must be a mistake to argue that the

---

* "And now, Israel, what doth the Lord thy God require of thee, but to fear the Lord thy God, to walk in His ways, and to love Him, and to serve the Lord thy God with all thy heart and with all thy soul, to keep His commandments and His statutes . . . And ye shall teach them to your children, speaking of them when thou sittest in thy house, and when thou walkest by the way, when thou liest down, and when thou risest up."—Deut. x. 12, xi. 19.

"Teach them thy sons, and thy sons' sons."—Deut. iv. 9.

"Ye *fathers*, provoke not your children to wrath."—Eph. vi. 4.

"*Fathers*, provoke not your children, that they be not discouraged."—Col. iii. 21.

exigencies of business or philanthropy are sufficient excuses for the very common practice of leaving everything to the mother or to outward agencies. Jean Paul Richter suggests to us the immense influence of fathers in the saying, " The words spoken by a father to his children in the privacy of home are not heard by the world, but, as in whispering galleries, they are clearly heard at the end, and by posterity."

A man and woman, together forming complete human nature, are required to make a home ; neither is the man without the woman, nor the woman without the man, in the training of the child—that holy work, the highest and noblest given to human creatures.

The thoughts expressed in this little volume do not claim originality; they are sent forth for the help of parents, who with small means and smaller leisure cannot avail themselves of the larger treatises on child training, in the hope that they may induce some to *think*. Thought is half way to doing.

> " Was never good work wrought
> Without beginning of good thought ? "

PART I.

The Rights of Children.

WHAT ARE THEY? FROM WHOM ARE THEY DEMANDED?

"Is it not an astonishing fact, that though on the treatment of offspring depend their lives and deaths and their moral welfare or ruin, yet not one word on the instruction of children is ever given to those who will be parents?"

HERBERT SPENCER.

"How shall we order the child, and how shall we do unto him?"—Judges xiii. 12.

The children's rights are :—

 (1). To be born into the world in a healthy condition. Parents are guilty of wilfully disregarding the laws of God who deny the power of pre-natal influences. The wrongs of children begin before birth. The weak body and weaker will, the diseases engendered

by drink and impurity, are handicapping tens
of thousands of lives for joyousness and use-
fulness in our land.

(2). Such a training as will fit them for spiritual,
mental, and physical life of the highest order.
That they may not be hindered, but helped in
coming to God; that good habits may be
formed; and that good health, which is
physical religion, may be developed by
judicious treatment.

(3). That the influence of good example shall
not be withheld.

From whom are these rights demanded? From
you who are parents. You are responsible for the
being of your children. Without your consent they
would not exist. To you, then, they must look for
their rights. You may hand over their education
to others, and imagine that with their clothing and
feeding your duties are fulfilled. But you are
mistaken: no one can do *your* work of training;
neglected by you, it must remain undone. The
period of childhood is short; time and opportunities
lost cannot be recalled. The work badly done
can never be done again.

This makes the work of parents of such

solemnity! What a fatal form of wrong-doing is slothfulness or ignorance! "Perhaps it is not too much to say that ninety-nine out of a hundred lost lives lie at the door of parents who took no pains to deliver their children from sloth, from sensual appetites, from wilfulness : no pains to fortify them with the habits of a good life."*

*Charlotte Mason.

The Need of Self-Training.

" Thou that teachest another, teachest thou not thyself ? "

God lays upon you as parents the duty of learning, by every possible means, the best way of fulfilling your responsibility. Not one in five thousand can be said to have native wisdom enough to train a child in the way he should go!

Parents, put yourselves to school again as teachers and scholars in one. In training your children you must needs first train yourself. The widest capacity and experience will here find scope, as the narrowest and smallest can be strengthened. Wisdom in training is not instinctive, although it is popularly supposed to be so. Natural affection, inspiring as it is, is not a sufficient qualification for parents. They need every help in their difficult work, and, above all, the " wisdom from above," which must be sought for daily guidance.

" If any man lack wisdom, let him ask of God."

It has been wisely said that " every father and mother should be as a skilled physician in the treatment of their children. As the physician needs accurate information, so do parents need an intelligent understanding of their children's characters before they can train them."

Few parents realise the complex nature of their children. Montaigne says, " It is not a soul, it is not a body we are training up, it is a man." The majority of fathers and mothers seem to forget that spirit, mind, and body equally live upon food and perish of famine ; all three require daily food. The bodies and minds of your children may be well nourished and well fed, while their spirits are starved and neglected. Could the spirit assume shape, what shrunken, pitiful shadows should we see in healthy bodies and cultivated minds!

Individuality of Children.

"Train up a child in the way he should go"; but, remember, every child is not meant to go into the same mould. A very common fault of parents is to strive to make each child conform to one pattern, perhaps to their own. There are no two children alike, no regulation stamp on the little ones. Earnest thought and prayer are required over each one, to develop the good and repress the evil. Your child is no sheet of white paper to write on, or wax to form as you choose. Each one comes with his special tendencies to good and evil, inherited from ancestors. He is a harp of a thousand strings, to be tuned and perfected for God's use and for the help of his fellows. Respect the *individuality* of your children. "A child is more than the mere child of his parents, he is an embryo man, with characteristics and qualities."*

* Trumbull.

Difference of Teaching and Training

———

To be quite clear on the matter of child-training as distinguished from education, some thought is required. Not a few confound the two, and perhaps this is the reason for the fact that, while *teachers* are in every way better prepared for their work of education at present than in past years, *parents* have not kept pace in that desire for knowledge which will better equip them for their duties. A well-known writer contrasts thus:—

> *Teaching* is causing another to *know*.
> *Training* is causing another to *do*.
> *Teaching* fills the mind.
> *Training* shapes the habits.
> *Teaching* may safely be handed over to others.
> *Training* is the special work of parents.*

———

* Trumbull,

Frequent Reason of Failure.

Christian parents desire ardently that, as their children grow up, they may be found coming forward to confess Christ, and are surprised if such is not the case. May not the secret be found in the fact that while pure and conscientious themselves, and with a lofty ideal for their offspring, they take no trouble, or are too ignorant, to foster and develop those traits of character which go to form such ideals?

If parents honestly watch themselves, they will discover the causes of their children's failings.

How significant are the words of the Lord Jesus Christ about the little ones:

" Take heed that ye offend not."

" Take heed that ye despise not."

" Take heed that ye hinder not."

One of the first laws of the science of education is that it depends on example. What parents *are* is more influential than what they *say*. It is in the exhibition of those qualities which are the fruit of the Spirit of God that parents will influence their

children's lives for good. The following pages,
therefore, deal with the spiritual first, putting fore-
most what is so often omitted in " Helps to Education." But, remembering the threefold nature of
the child, hints upon his mental and physical well-
being are included, with the prayer that parents
(those members of the community who have more
influence on the future of the race than any other)
may here find some help and encouragement.
Courage and patience are necessary; your children
are worth it. So great a work cannot be achieved
without a struggle. But what of that, if the
memory of your purity and love keeps your son from
sinning, and your tender warnings follow your
daughter into the tide of vanity and keep her in the
hour of peril? Grace is given for this work of
child training. " And grace, given and used, means
an exceeding great reward."

Pray constantly for this grace, that you may
be able to teach your children how to " live " in
the fullest sense of the word. The first recorded
prayer in God's Word is that of a father for his
son, "Oh, that Ishmael might live before Thee!"
(Gen. xvii. 18). Parents are more than friends and
advisers; they have promised to them and to their

children the gift of the Holy Spirit. Parents, *you* are to train your sons and daughters for the Kingdom of God. You are God's appointed ministers to them. *You* must lead them to the Cross. You must help them, in the midst of temptation, to practise that self-denial which the Saviour links with the Cross. God grant that all who read may know some day the joy of saying, " Behold ! Lord, here am I, and the children which Thou hast given me."

PART II.

SPIRIT.

"Do not teach your child that he *is* a body and *has* a spirit; teach him rather that he *is* a spirit and *has* a body."

GEORGE MACDONALD.

"The fruit of the Spirit is love—joy—peace—long-suffering—gentleness—goodness—faithfulness—meekness—temperance (self-control)."

"*Love* is true life and strength,
Joy is love exulting,
Peace is love in repose,
Longsuffering is love on trial,
Gentleness is love overflowing,
Goodness is love in action,
Faith is love receiving,
Meekness is love at school.
Temperance is love in training."

Love.

"Love is of God. He that loveth not knoweth not God, for God is love."—1 John iv. 7-8.

Love is always self-surrender and sacrifice.

Human love, however sacred, may perish.

Parents, see that you feed that flame of love which

c

God has kindled between you and your children; warm your home with the fire of love.

Unkind words, harsh judgments issuing from parents' lips poison the sweet waters of home life.

Seek to maintain the rule of love as a principle, not fitfully, as instinct suggests.

Do not be afraid of telling your children you love them. Some would die for them, but would not tell them so with loving sympathy.

By your love draw your children to God. Love inspires, and inspiration is the secret of training.

Watch and pray against every sign of selfish or unloving spirit in your children, as a seed which will bear bitter fruit.

Joy.

"For joy that a man is born into the world."—John xvi. 21

The spirit of thanksgiving is a good preparation for child-training.

Sunshine in the sky is delightful and desirable so, also, is sunshine in the home.

To make happiness around does not require much sacrifice on the part of parents, but it requires tact, and study, and practice.

It is very easy to darken the outlook of the little ones. Endeavour, therefore, to provide an atmosphere of joyfulness. Good qualities grow more quickly in sunshine than in shade.

"Joy is a thing to be practised, like the violin."

Present Christ to your child as the Joy-giver. This is an attractive aspect to him; teach him true religion has nothing to do with melancholy countenances and mournful tones.

If you despond and complain, you darken lives.

Frobel attaches great importance to singing with children. "A merry heart doeth good, like medicine."

True reverence is shown better in gladness than in storm.

Peace.

"Follow peace with all men. —Heb. xii. 14

Parents who are themselves restless and in-harmonious cannot make an atmosphere of peace and they are responsible, to a great extent, for the serenity of the home.

Unless you keep your own childhood in mind, it is difficult to realise how a sharp tone will rankle.

Let your commands be given in quiet, deliberate tones. Self-rule is the secret of all rule.

The atmosphere of the home is all-important to child growth, and the ungenial chills of criticism and fault-finding are as injurious to his development as the " explosive storm-bursts of passion."

The secret of the Spirit of Peace is given to those who do the will of Christ, whose life is hidden with God. It is not very common, even among Christians. Cultivate, therefore, if only for the sake of your children, that serene spirit which stays itself upon God.

Long-Suffering (Patience).

"Ye have need of patience.' —Heb. x. 36.

God dealeth with you as with sons; that is, He is long-suffering, not easily provoked.

Does your love for your child lead you to "bear all things, endure all things?"

Put yourself in the children's place; remember the time when you were young; do not expect them to be as perfect as yourself—or to be able to begin life with all the experience which years have given to you.

Take time to listen to the childish griefs and sorrows. Hasty and unjust judgments on the part of parents injure children's temper. Help and encouragement they all need. Hastiness of all kinds must be avoided.

Have patience with your growing boys and girls in the transition period between childhood and maturity. Many excellent people are yet fretful, irascible, peevish, sullen—in fact, ill-tempered; not that they were born so, but because they were allowed to grow up in an atmosphere of impatience.

Watch patiently and hopefully for good in your children, and be not too much cast down by failure. "Who knows the end?"

Gentleness.

" Thy gentleness hath made me great.'
" The wisdom that is from above is first pure,
then peaceable, gentle . . ."—James iii. 3-17.

Parents must rule by love, not by fear.

Train your child's will gently; do not speak of breaking it. A child with a broken will will be worse equipped for life than if he had a broken leg. You cannot force him to choose the right. God holds sacred the personality of every human creature, and by gentle means He *invites*, but does not force.

Brute force may compel a child to yield his will to his father, but it does not train that will. Untruthfulness is not seldom caused by fear of violent parents.

Scolding is always out of place.

Many good parents scold their children, but if they will omit the scolding tone, and gently and calmly point out the nature and consequences of the fault, they will find that more is done for their characters, without the loss of sympathy, which comes of cross, uncontrolled tones.

Goodness.

"Depart from evil and do good."—Ps. xxxiv. 14.

"Let your children learn early that if they would see *good* it will be found with God."

You must *get* before you can give. "They first gave their own selves to the Lord."

Worldly, slothful, careless parents cannot train souls for God.

Your own feet must be upon the Rock before you can stretch down a hand to the little one to clasp in climbing.

Yours is the duty of revealing God to your child. If you tell him God only loves *good* children, but not bad ones, he may think, when his conduct is good, that he has merited God's love. Tell him that God loves all, but is *grieved* with the wicked.

Pray not only *for*, but *with* your children. Let them hear your voice speaking to God for them.

Teach them to pray for what they want as a child coming to a father, who is waiting to hear.

Expect your children to be good. Lay most stress on the good in their characters; encourage them by praise to be good.

Meekness.

"Blessed are the meek." "Learn of Me, for I am meek and lowly of heart."—Matt. xi. 29.

The parents' voices are the barometers of the family peace. Children catch imperious tones very quickly. Why use arbitrary and threatening manners, when a calm, quiet request will gain obedience?

" Meekness is maintaining peace and patience in the midst of pelting provocations."

Meekness must be both active and passive ; it must lead us to subdue our own resentments, and bear patiently with the passions and resentments of our children.

You may irritate a child by boasting of your superior conduct when of his age. The self-applause of many parents is a stumbling-block to their children.

Do not retain your anger or "bear a grudge" against your growing girls and boys. Beware of nagging them.

Sarcasm, also, is a dangerous weapon to use, and scoffs and jeers from parents are destructive of influence.

Faithfulness.

***

"It is required of a man that he be found faithful."—1 Co. iv. 2.

***

If there is any cruelty in the world which is truly terrible in its consequences, it is that worked by selfish, indulgent, unfaithful parents.

It was parental faithfulness in Abraham upon which God put such honour—" he commanded his household, and his children after him, that they should keep the way of the Lord."

Are you consistent with your profession? Who so quick to detect inconsistency as a child?

Show your faithfulness by shunning no part of child-training which is difficult.

A dangerous silence on the subject of purity is kept by parents; they impress the duties of honesty, sobriety, and industry upon their children, but the duty of purity of life is never mentioned.*

How can we expect the young to stand firm in the hour of temptation unless they are forewarned, and so forearmed? If you find it difficult to speak, read Exodus iv. 10 to 12.

---

* See "Purity," page 34.

D

Temperance (Self-Control).

If parents honestly watch themselves, they will discover often in their own impulses and tempers the causes of their children's failings.

To govern ourselves is the preliminary for ruling our children. Self-mastery is the goal at which training aims, and it is for parents to decide whether in after years the child shall be a slave to himself or master of himself.

A child may be a true man in self-mastery, if well trained in self-control.

A very common form of want of self-control is found in hasty punishment, not for the fault of disobedience, but for an accident brought about by the fault; a precious object is lost or broken, the father or mother fly into a passion and punish. The child suffers for what he had no intention of doing, but the disobedience, the wilful fault, is ignored.

We are too much inclined to estimate guilt by immediate consequences.

PART III.

MIND.

"The mind of man is like a mill, which will grind whatever you put into it, whether it be husk or wheat. The Devil is very eager to have his turn at this mill, and to employ it for grinding the husk of vain thoughts. Keep the wheat of the Word in the mind."

WILLIAMS OF WERN

Discipline.

"Thou shalt consider in thine heart that, as a man chasteneth his son, so the Lord thy God chasteneth thee."—Deut. viii. 5.

Family discipline has a divine warrant.

1. It must be *intelligent*. Take pains to understand your children, and you will have less to punish.

2. It must be *gentle*. Beware of violence, passion, and publicity. Do not punish in the presence of others.

3. It must be *firm*. *Love* may undermine *Law*. Love and law must be equal factors in child

discipline. Moral cowardice hinders many a parent, and makes family discipline feeble that should be firm. Father and mother must be of one mind in the matter.

4. It must be *just*. It must not be partial—have no pets; nor prolonged—forgive your children as soon as they repent.

5. It must be given in the spirit of Christ. Let the children know you punish them because you are bound to by God's command. You dare not let them go unrestrained. Tell them of Eli and his sons.

Reasonable Obedience.

"If ye be willing and obedient, ye shall eat the good of the land."—Isaiah i. 19.

Take time and trouble to explain the "why" and "wherefore" of discipline, and thus seek to make your children fellow workers with yourself in the formation of their own characters.

Boys and girls are eminently reasonable beings, and resent arbitrary commands.

Do not judge your child's conduct from the standpoint of your own. Endeavour to see through his eyes, and with his experience, before you judge him.

Tell a child constantly that he is "naughty," it is but reasonable to believe that he will live up to his reputation.

Let there be no suspicion of antagonism between yourself and your children; beware of being "enemy-friend;" and use your reason if you would gain obedience.

1. When you give a command, see that it is obeyed.

2. Do not give several at once, or continually pester the child with "do this" or "don't do that." The chronic "don't" of the parent brings the chronic "wont" of the child.

3. Do not command what you cannot enforce.

4. Do not bully your children into submission.

5. When once a thing is forbidden, *keep your word*.

Sympathy.

"Be ye kind one to another—tender-hearted."—Eph. iv. 32.

A child needs sympathy as much as he does love. "Ten are loved where one is sympathised with."

Lack of sympathy on the part of parents is a cause of great unhappiness in families, and yet there is no surer way of gaining the ear of your children than by sympathising with their joys and sorrows, lessons, and play; every true child *needs* it.

Parents, if you feel that sympathy is not easy to show, cultivate it diligently: remember, if you lose opportunities of showing it, your children will turn to strangers; for sympathy they will have.

By this bond of sympathy mothers can gain their girls' confidence, fathers can enter into the life of his boys, difficult ways are made smoother.

Have sympathy with your children's tastes. If they have a bent for any one thing, do not try to quench it.

If your boy or girl come to you for advice, enter as far as possible into their wishes; if impracticable, sympathise with their disappointment.

If religious doubts arise, do not try to stamp them out by severity; talk matters over, and show your sympathy with difficulties.

Self-denial.

"Endure hardness as a good soldier of Jesus Christ."
—2 Timothy ii. 3.

The benefits of self-denial are great in child-training.

It is the duty of every parent to deny a child in many things which he wants; thus he is trained in self-denial and endurance; it is positively cruel to give him all he asks for.

The grace of "doing without" can be taught best by example. No habit of self-denial for others will impoverish your life.

Self-denial is a virtue seldom attained except by early domestic training; if a child is allowed from infancy to indulge his own impulses and wishes, regardless of the good of others, there is small chance that he will master them in manhood.

To know ourselves as a help to others is an honest source of joy.

Spare no effort to cultivate generosity towards others, a methodical self-denial for the poor and for God's work at home and abroad.

When selfishness is exhibited, do not lecture or scold, rather picture some hero who has opposite traits of character. Speak of noble men and women who have endured hardness.

Imagination.

"We know in part, we prophesy in part."—1 Cor. xiii. 9.

Imagination expands the mind by expanding the boundary of thought.

Not a few parents repress imagination in their children, thinking it evil; whereas, rightly guarded, it has a most important part in training.

By the power of his imagination, man's thought rises to God; he is able to enter into the feelings of others; by the use of imagination the arts and sciences are advanced, for it is a constituent part of inventions, pictures, music, etc.

Guard sacredly your children's imaginative powers; learn to distinguish between the *fanciful* and the *false*. The last, which poses as truth, is hurtful, but the fanciful is known to be beyond human experience, and does not deceive. This is why fairy stories are not hurtful, but exciting tales of false adventure are.

Inspire your child's imagination by tales of heroism, and let your heroes be of the *homely* sort, that the daily common life may be raised by thoughts of noble deeds.

E

Purity.

"Whatsoever things are pure—think on these things."
—Phil. iv. 8.

"Be pure, and thou must needs be brave."

A wide and half-concealed immorality lies just beneath the surface of society. "A precipice lies before every boy and girl when they emerge from the shelter of home; but a sure, safe path leads round it. We must gently warn them of the one, we must lead them to the other."

Parents, your silence is dangerous; set up a habit of confidence with your children, that you may the more easily warn them of so vital a danger.

Do not be shocked or angry when your boy utters some half ignorant remark or question. Here is your opportunity for instruction! Let their first knowledge of this evil come from a pure source.

Speak of the dignity of the body, which may become a temple of the Holy Ghost. Tell of the wonderful relationship between mother and child, in the absolute union of their two lives in one body. Teach them the profanity of light and vain thoughts about love and marriage. Teach your boys to honour womanhood, the degradation of which *is sin*, and will surely bring punishment.

Friendship.

"Thine own friend and thy father's friend forsake not."
—Prov. xxvii. 10

Show your children that you are their best friend, as well as assert it.

As your boys and girls grow up, put off to some extent parental authority, and make them your confidants as to income, plans, etc.; let them feel you regard their co-operation, and even advice, as worth having.

Teach your children that friendship is one of God's most precious gifts, not to be lightly entered into. Encourage them to make friends, and give them opportunities of meeting.

Watch carefully the companions they choose, and discourage fickleness; teach that "a man that hath friends must show himself friendly."

Friendship is more or less at the basis of every other relation in life. One of the best things that can be said about parents is that they are the *friends* of their children.

Lay much stress on the Friendship of Christ, as a guard and guide for the young.

Citizenship.

" Thou shalt love thy neighbour as thyself."—Luke x 27.

Love to our neighbours leads us to care for the welfare of others.

To take an interest in the right government of our country, to be willing to serve for the public good, should be taught to children as a privilege as well as a duty.

Cultivate in your children all generous and honest feelings. Expect from your girls, equally with your boys, an interest in public life—public business, committees, elections, Poor Law meetings, speeches, County and District Councils. These do not sound romantic, but they mean much social prosperity. Educate sons and daughters to give the vote intelligently. Tell them to do so with the desire to diminish the sum of human misery.

All, if they choose, may be brave and patriotic. Time, work, and courage are more than money. Thought and love for others are worth more than gold.

Amusements.

Body and mind alike require recreation; neither good health nor wisdom is possible without it.

The aim of parents should be to find such recreations for their children which shall invigorate spirit, mind, and body. Time spent in games is not lost.

Much of the so-called amusement of the present day is absolutely exhausting ; the laborious Sunday outing ; the dance carried on until early morning ; the athletics which require the Sunday to be spent in bed to recuperate.

The theatre and the music hall—places where the senses are stirred, the passions fired, and the deadly drink furnished—are not the places for your boys and girls. Good rules for the guidance of parents as to amusements are the following tests. Amusements are wrong which

(1). Render work distasteful.

(2). Damage the desire for divine things.

(3). Are purchased by the moral loss of those who amuse.

Direct your children's minds to simple pleasure, cultivate the sense of beauty in scenery, in trees and flowers, birds and insects, river and sea, sun, moon, and stars.

Do not grudge a day spent with them in the country.

Manners.

"Be courteous." "Manners makyth manne." Good manners are more attractive than beauty of face.

Parents, remember your example; if you drop your manners to them, can you expect the children to do otherwise?

The atmosphere of courtesy must be created by father and mother, who will require tact, constant vigilance, and patience to that end.

Do not fail to train the young in *home* courtesies— the placing of a chair, opening of a door, the attentive eye and ear at table; rendering services such as these nourish love.

Avoid disagreeable topics, jokes upon personal and mental infirmities; be careful of the feelings of relations. Why do people push and scramble for the best places, why do they snatch and bang doors, interrupt and contradict? Because self is first with them. Teach the young ones never to lose a chance of giving pleasure to others.

Good manners have been defined as an "unselfish regard for the feelings of others."

Conversation.

"Be thou an example . . . in conversation."—1 Tim. iv. 12.

Few parents realise the formative power of conversation on the young mind.

How different would be the table talk in homes if we could realise the influence of words and opinions on our boys and girls.

Let meal times be opportunities for getting at the minds of your children. The culture of the judgment, of right views of life, of allowance for the faults of others, may go on at table, or, on the contrary, evil speaking, gossip, and quarrelling may here find a fine field.

Parents, display your tact in leading your children's conversation. Do not lecture, or show that you are talking to improve their minds: they resent this. Store up from day to day topics of conversation.

Do not allow free criticism of the food provided.

Let your children know that "*idle*" as well as profane words are seeds which will bear bitter fruit.

"The first ingredient of good talk is *truth;* the next, *good sense;* the third, *good humour:* the fourth, *wit.*"

PART IV.

BODY.

"Let thy mind's sweetness have its operation upon thy body, clothes, and habitation."

Health

"Good health is physical religion."

"It is not merely selfish, but wasteful, to throw it away."

Health is very much a matter of good habits.

Fresh air, sufficient exercise, moderation in eating, plenty of water, outside and in, total abstinence from intoxicants, mean much to the comfort of life.

Give Nature fair play, and let her alone. Parents, do not be frequently dosing the children with drugs. Patent medicines, so largely used, make pockets light, but heads heavy.

Over strain and over pressure mean eventually weakness and irritability.

F

Excitement, worry, and self-indulgence kill more than hard work.

Watch your children, if fretful and troublesome; they, in all probability, require change and fresh air.

Our climate demands woollen underclothing. By its aid chills are prevented and temperature preserved.

Food.

Consider the amount of ill-temper, despondency, and general unhappiness caused by indigestion, and you will agree that this is an important topic for the consideration of parents.

A human creature needs food, if he is to perform his daily work, as much as an engine does coal and water. The young need more food in proportion than the mature, and they need to take it oftener than adults. The building up of the child by what he eats is of such importance that the parent must see that no whims or fancies of the child interfere with his proper nourishment.

The errors committed in the feeding of infants
are legion, but perhaps the greatest is the substitu-
tion of soaked bread and biscuit for milk food before
the age of six months. Tens of thousands die annually
of this mistaken feeding. You may stuff your baby
with food while in reality you are starving him, for
the child cannot digest such food until his teeth
begin to appear. Keep to milk and water if you wish
your child to thrive. The craving for solid food is
a sign of indigestion on the part of infants. Milk
is standard diet, and furnishes all that an infant requires.

Total Abstinence.

It is the duty of parents to learn the truth about
alcohol.

On medical authority we know that not one of
the "wrongs, physical or mental, is more surely
passed on to those unborn than the wrongs trans-
mitted by alcohol."

Honest water never made any one a sinner, but crime may almost be said to be concentrated alcohol.

"Where Satan cannot go in person," says an old Jewish proverb, "he sends wine."

Parents, be on the safe side; though you feel yourself safe, you cannot ensure safety for your children unless you teach them to abstain, not only by precept but by example.

Two thousand medical men of the United Kingdom, many of the highest distinction, have made the declaration—

(1). That a very large portion of misery, poverty, disease, and crime is induced by strong drink.

(2). That the most perfect health is compatible with total abstinence.

(3). That persons accustomed to drink intoxicants may with perfect safety discontinue them.

(4) That total and universal abstinence will contribute to the health and happiness of the human race.

Fresh Air.

The importance of a sufficient supply of pure air to our well-being and to our actual existence cannot be over-estimated.

It has been said that the majority of diseases which afflict human creatures are due to impure and unwholesome or poisoned air.

Air which has been breathed has lost some of its life-giving power ; we had better avoid taking it into our lungs. If it were anything else but air we should be disgusted at the very idea of using it second-hand after its ejection by people not too clean.

Your children are more dependent upon fresh air even than you are, therefore see to ventilation as one of the primary necessities of life.

The air of rooms cannot be kept as pure as the outside atmosphere, but much may be done. In bedrooms the fireplace must always be left open, the windows should pull down from the top. Close bedroom air has been known to produce consumption and scrofula.

Change of air is very beneficial in many diseases.

Rest.

The cry for rest has always been louder even than the cry for food. The best rest comes from sound sleep. Sleep will restore vigour to an overworked brain, build up a weak body, cure a headache, and a long list of nervous maladies which here cannot be mentioned.

The mind is strengthened and the senses more acute after rest. If you want a healthy mind in a healthy body to characterise your children, see to it that they obtain sufficient rest.

Ten to twelve hours' sleep are required by a child in winter, while seven or eight hours are sufficient for the adult. "One hour's sleep before midnight is worth two after."

Obedience and punctuality are requisite if children are to have proper time for rest.

If your child is weak, make his rest during the day obligatory. Heart and lungs are helped by the horizontal position. Growing children often require to lie down.

Avoid opiates of all kinds; their use causes cerebral congestion, only differing in amount from the condition which naturally issues in death.

Dress.

In all ranks of life the human heart yearns for the beautiful.

As dress is absolutely necessary, and is also a medium of pleasure, or the reverse, it is important that the children be trained to exercise taste and discretion in respect to it.

To be beautifully and gracefully dressed is a right instinct. It is not wrong to wish to look lovely.

Unfortunately, *beauty* and *grace* are often interpreted to mean, richness and brilliance, both of which are needless in good dressing. Parents, teach your children some rules by which they may dress well.

(1). *Suitability*. What is suitable to age, position in life, earnings, work, climate.

(2). *Simplicity*. Showy and extravagant dress is of the worst taste. Tight lacing and high heels are positively to be discouraged as dangerous to health; the wearing of birds and aigrettes is costly of life, and is cruelty.

(3). *Harmony.* The whole person, under-clothing, boots, every article must be clean and sufficient. The choice of colours, the arrangement of hair, all produce harmony.

Parents, train your children to be as careful of the cleanliness and neatness of their dress for home wear as for out of doors. Expect this as part of the " honour " due to you, and show that you appreciate their efforts in this direction by judicious praise.

Lemmon & Son, Ltd., Printers, 42, Lower Road, S.E.

www.ingramcontent.com/pod-product-compliance
Lightning Source LLC
Chambersburg PA
CBHW081303040426
42452CB00014B/2630